Scott
Science

See learning in a whole new light

Editorial Offices: Glenview, Illinois • Parsippany, New Jersey • New York, New York
Sales Offices: Boston, Massachusetts • Duluth, Georgia • Glenview, Illinois
Coppell, Texas • Sacramento, California • Mesa, Arizona

Series Authors

Dr. Timothy Cooney
Professor of Earth Science and Science Education
University of Northern Iowa (UNI)
Cedar Falls, Iowa

Dr. Jim Cummins
Professor
Department of Curriculum, Teaching, and Learning
University of Toronto
Toronto, Canada

Dr. James Flood
Distinguished Professor of Literacy and Language
School of Teacher Education
San Diego State University
San Diego, California

Barbara Kay Foots, M.Ed.
Science Education Consultant
Houston, Texas

Dr. M. Jenice Goldston
Associate Professor of Science Education
Department of Elementary Education Programs
University of Alabama
Tuscaloosa, Alabama

Dr. Shirley Gholston Key
Associate Professor of Science Education
Instruction and Curriculum Leadership Department
College of Education
University of Memphis
Memphis, Tennessee

Dr. Diane Lapp
Distinguished Professor of Reading and Language Arts in Teacher Education
San Diego State University
San Diego, California

Sheryl A. Mercier
Classroom Teacher
Dunlap Elementary School
Dunlap, California

Dr. Karen L. Ostlund
Director
UTeach, College of Natural Sciences
The University of Texas at Austin
Austin, Texas

Dr. Nancy Romance
Professor of Science Education & Principal Investigator
NSF/IERI Science IDEAS Project
Charles E. Schmidt College of Science
Florida Atlantic University
Boca Raton, Florida

Dr. William Tate
Chair and Professor of Education and Applied Statistics
Department of Education
Washington University
St. Louis, Missouri

Dr. Kathryn C. Thornton
Professor
School of Engineering and Applied Science
University of Virginia
Charlottesville, Virginia

Dr. Leon Ukens
Professor of Science Education
Department of Physics, Astronomy, and Geosciences
Towson University
Towson, Maryland

Steve Weinberg
Consultant
Connecticut Center for Advanced Technology
East Hartford, Connecticut

ISBN: 0-328-10001-3 (SVE); ISBN: 0-328-15671-X (A); ISBN: 0-328-15677-9 (B);
ISBN: 0-328-15683-3 (C); ISBN: 0-328-15689-2 (D)

Consulting Author

Dr. Michael P. Klentschy
Superintendent
El Centro Elementary School District
El Centro, California

Science Content Consultants

Dr. Frederick W. Taylor
Senior Research Scientist
Institute for Geophysics
Jackson School of Geosciences
The University of Texas at Austin
Austin, Texas

Dr. Ruth E. Buskirk
Senior Lecturer
School of Biological Sciences
The University of Texas at Austin
Austin, Texas

Dr. Cliff Frohlich
Senior Research Scientist
Institute for Geophysics
Jackson School of Geosciences
The University of Texas at Austin
Austin, Texas

Brad Armosky
McDonald Observatory
The University of Texas at Austin
Austin, Texas

Content Consultants

Adena Williams Loston, Ph.D.
Chief Education Officer
Office of the Chief Education Officer

Clifford W. Houston, Ph.D.
*Deputy Chief Education Officer
for Education Programs*
Office of the Chief Education Officer

Frank C. Owens
Senior Policy Advisor
Office of the Chief Education Officer

Deborah Brown Biggs
Manager, Education Flight Projects Office
Space Operations Mission Directorate, Education Lead

Erika G. Vick
*NASA Liaison to
Pearson Scott Foresman*
Education Flight Projects Office

William E. Anderson
*Partnership Manager
for Education*
Aeronautics Research Mission Directorate

Anita Krishnamurthi
Program Planning Specialist
Space Science Education and Outreach Program

Bonnie J. McClain
Chief of Education
Exploration Systems Mission Directorate

Diane Clayton, Ph.D.
Program Scientist
Earth Science Education

Deborah Rivera
Strategic Alliances Manager
Office of Public Affairs
NASA Headquarters

Douglas D. Peterson
*Public Affairs Officer,
Astronaut Office*
Office of Public Affairs
NASA Johnson Space Center

Nicole Cloutier
*Public Affairs Officer,
Astronaut Office*
Office of Public Affairs
NASA Johnson Space Center

Dr. Jennifer J. Wiseman
*Hubble Space Telescope
Program Scientist*
NASA Headquarters

Reviewers

Science

See learning in a whole new light

Unit A Life Science

What do living things need?

Chapter 1 • Living and Nonliving

Chapter 2 • Habitats

Where
plants a
animals

Life Science

Chapter 3 • How Plants and Animals Live

Chapter 4 • Life Cycles

How do animals and plants grow and change?

Unit A Life Science

How are living things connected?

Chapter 5 • Food Chains

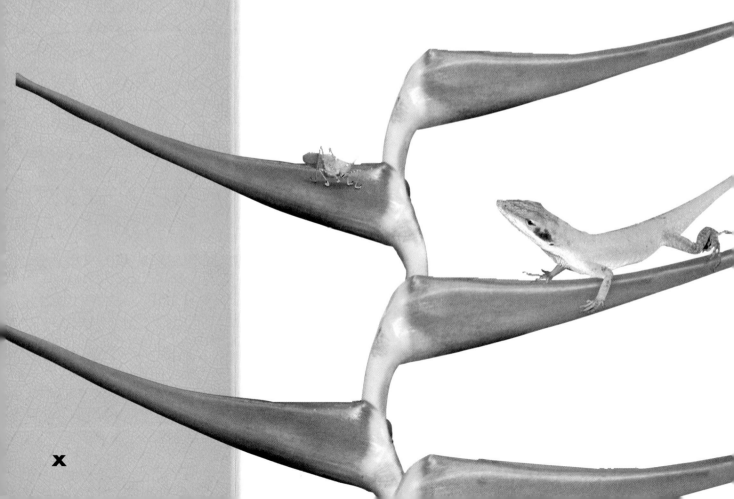

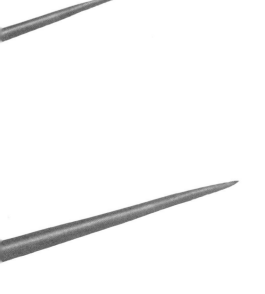

How are land, water, and air important?

Chapter 6 • Land, Water, and Air

WE RECYCLE

Chapter 7 • Weather

What are the four seasons?

Unit C Physical Science

How can objects be described?

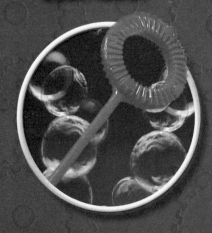

Chapter 8 • Observing Matter

Chapter 9 • Movement and Sound

What makes objects move?

Unit C · Physical Science

Where does energy come from?

Chapter 10 • Learning About Energy

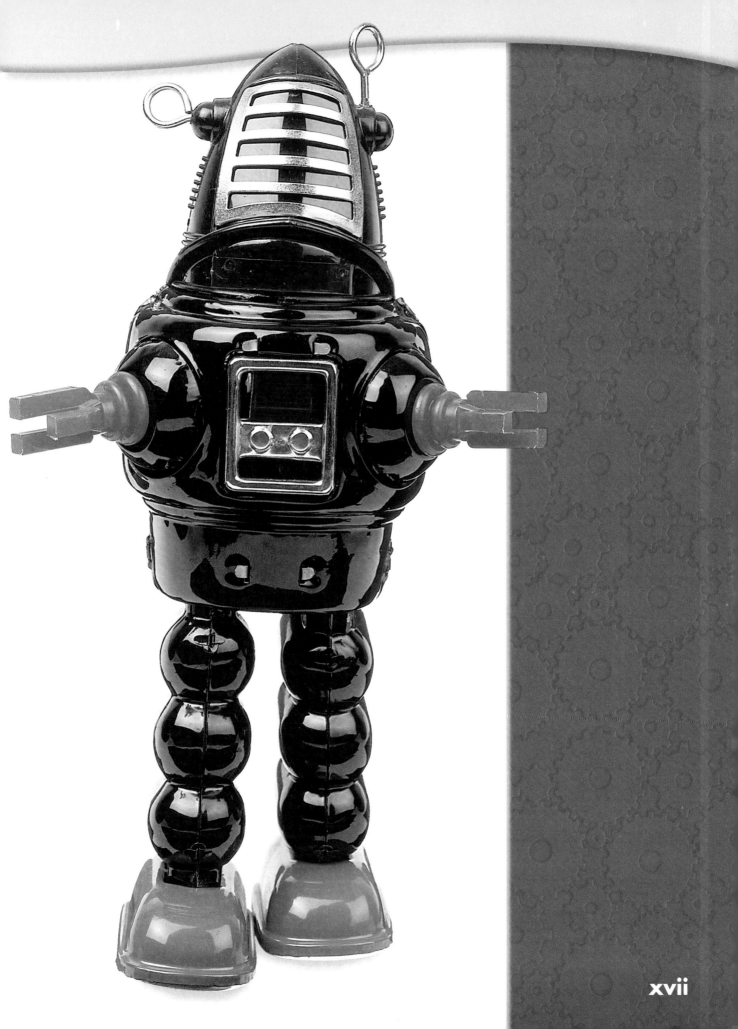

Unit D Space and Technology

What is in the sky?

Chapter 12 • Science in Our World

How does technology help people?

How to Read Science

Each chapter in your book has a page like this one. This page shows you how to use a reading skill.

Before reading
First, read the Build Background page. Next, read the How To Read Science page. Then, think about what you already know. Last, make a list of what you already know.

Target Reading Skill
The target reading skill will help you understand what you read.

Real-World Connection
Each page has an example of something you will learn.

Graphic Organizer
A graphic organizer can help you think about what you learn.

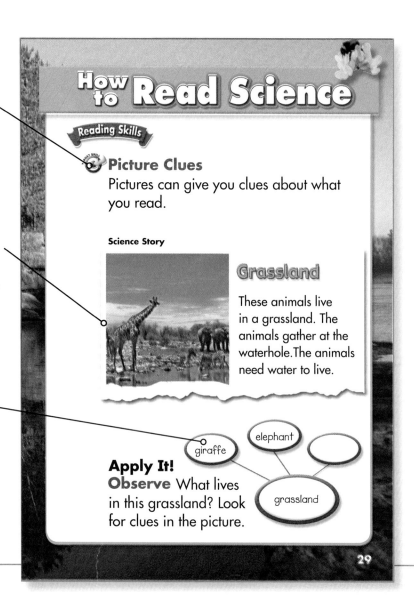

How to Read Science

Reading Skills

Picture Clues
Pictures can give you clues about what you read.

Science Story

Grassland

These animals live in a grassland. The animals gather at the waterhole. The animals need water to live.

Apply It!
Observe What lives in this grassland? Look for clues in the picture.

elephant
giraffe
grassland

Map Facts
A swamp is a wetland. Okefenokee Swamp in Georgia has about 70 islands.

crane

dragonfly

bullfrog

✓ **Lesson Checkpoint**
1. What does a duck get in a wetland?
2. Use **picture clues** to tell what animals live in a wetland.

35

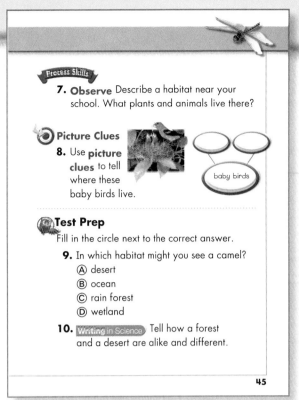

Process Skills

7. **Observe** Describe a habitat near your school. What plants and animals live there?

Picture Clues
8. Use **picture clues** to tell where these baby birds live.

baby birds

Test Prep
Fill in the circle next to the correct answer.
9. In which habitat might you see a camel?
   Ⓐ desert
   Ⓑ ocean
   Ⓒ rain forest
   Ⓓ wetland
10. Writing in Science Tell how a forest and a desert are alike and different.

45

During reading
Use the checkpoint as you read the lesson. This will help you check how much you understand.

After reading
Think about what you have learned. Compare what you learned with the list you made before you read the chapter. Answer the questions in the Chapter Review.

Target Reading Skills

These are some target reading skills that appear in this book.

- Cause and Effect
- Alike and Different
- Put Things in Order
- Predict

- Draw Conclusions
- Picture Clues
- Important Details

Science Process Skills

Observe

A scientist who wants to find out about the ocean observes many things. You use your senses to find out about things too.

Classify

Scientists classify living things in the ocean. You classify when you sort or group things by their properties.

Estimate and Measure

Scientists can estimate the size of living things in the ocean. This means they make a careful guess about the size or amount of something. Then they measure it.

Infer

Scientists are always learning about living things in the ocean. Scientists draw a conclusion or make a guess from what they already know.

Under the Water

Scientists use process skills to find out about things. You will use these skills when you do the activities in this book. Suppose scientists want to learn about living things in the ocean. Which process skills might they use?

Predict

Scientists tell what they think they will find before they go into the ocean.

Make and Use Models

Scientists might make and use models. Models show what they already know.

Make Definitions

Scientists use what they know to tell what something means.

Science Process Skills

Make Hypotheses
Think of a question you have about living things in the ocean. Make a statement that you can test to answer your question.

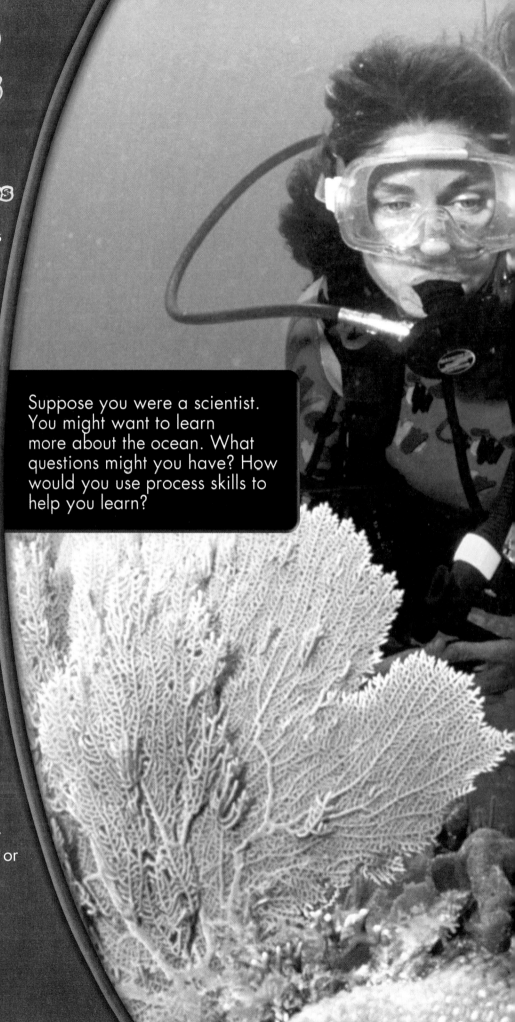

Suppose you were a scientist. You might want to learn more about the ocean. What questions might you have? How would you use process skills to help you learn?

Collect Data
Scientists record what they observe and measure. Scientists put this data into charts or graphs.

Interpret Data
Scientists use what they learn to solve problems or answer questions.

Investigate and Experiment
Scientists plan and do an investigation as they study the ocean.

Control Variables
Scientists plan a fair test. Scientists change only one thing in their test. Scientists keep everything else the same.

Communicate
Scientists tell what they learn about living things in the ocean.

Using Scientific Methods

Scientific methods are ways of finding answers. Scientific methods have these steps. Sometimes scientists do the steps in a different order. Scientists do not always do all of the steps.

Ask a question.

Ask a question that you want answered.

Do seeds need water to grow?

Make your hypothesis.

Tell what you think the answer is to your question.

If seeds are watered, then they will grow.

Plan a fair test.

Change only one thing.

Keep everything else the same.

Water one pot with seeds.

no water

water

Do your test.

Test your hypothesis. Do your test more than once. See if your results are the same.

Collect and record your data.

Keep records of what you find out. Use words or drawings to help.

Tell your conclusion.

Observe the results of your test. Decide if your hypothesis is right or wrong. Tell what you decide.

Seeds need water to grow.

no water

water

Go further.

Use what you learn. Think of new questions or better ways to do a test.

Ask a Question

Make Your Hypothesis

Plan a Fair Test

Do Your Test

Collect and Record Your Data

Tell Your Conclusion

Go Further

Science Tools

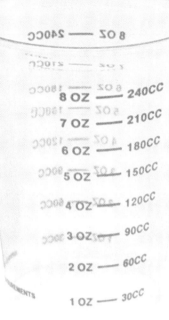

8 OZ	240CC
7 OZ	210CC
6 OZ	180CC
5 OZ	150CC
4 OZ	120CC
3 OZ	90CC
2 OZ	60CC
1 OZ	30CC

Scientists use many different kinds of tools.

Measuring cup
You can use a measuring cup to measure volume. Volume is how much space something takes up.

Stopwatch
A stopwatch measures how much time something takes.

Computer
You can learn about science at a special Internet website. Go to www.sfsuccessnet.com.

Ruler
You can use a ruler to measure how long something is. Most scientists use a ruler to measure length in centimeters or millimeters.

Thermometer

A thermometer measures the temperature. When the temperature gets warmer, the red line moves up. When it gets cooler, the red line moves down. Most thermometers have a Celsius and Fahrenheit scale. Most scientists use the Celsius scale.

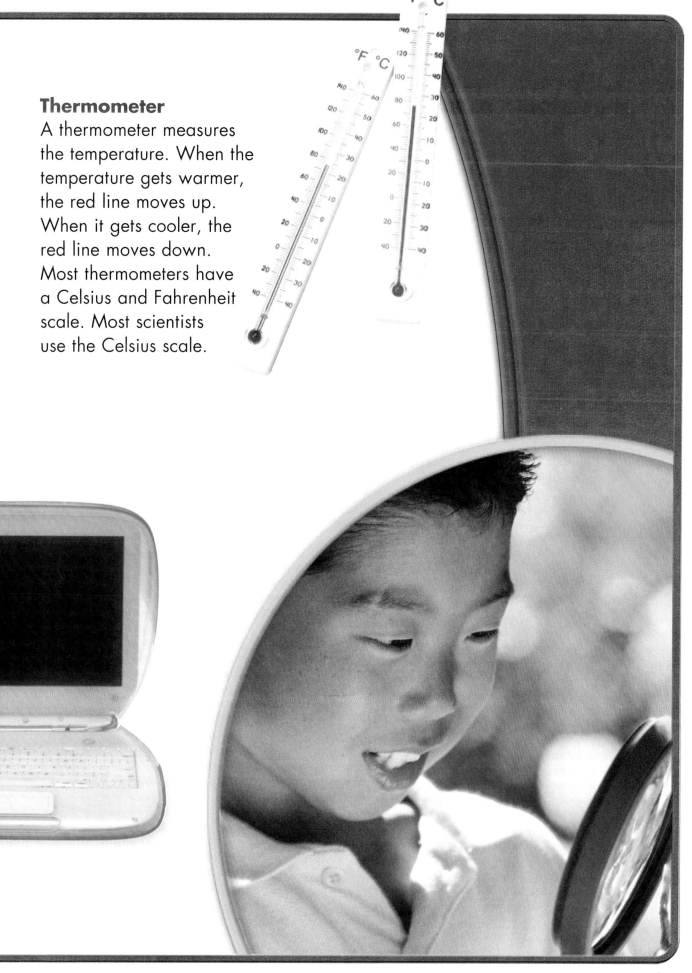

Science Tools

Safety goggles
You can use safety goggles to protect your eyes.

Calculator
A calculator can help you do things, such as add and subtract.

Balance
A balance is used to measure the mass of objects. Mass is how much matter an object has. Most scientists measure mass in grams or kilograms.

Meterstick
You can use a meterstick to measure how long something is too. Scientists use a meterstick to measure in meters.

Clock
A clock measures time.

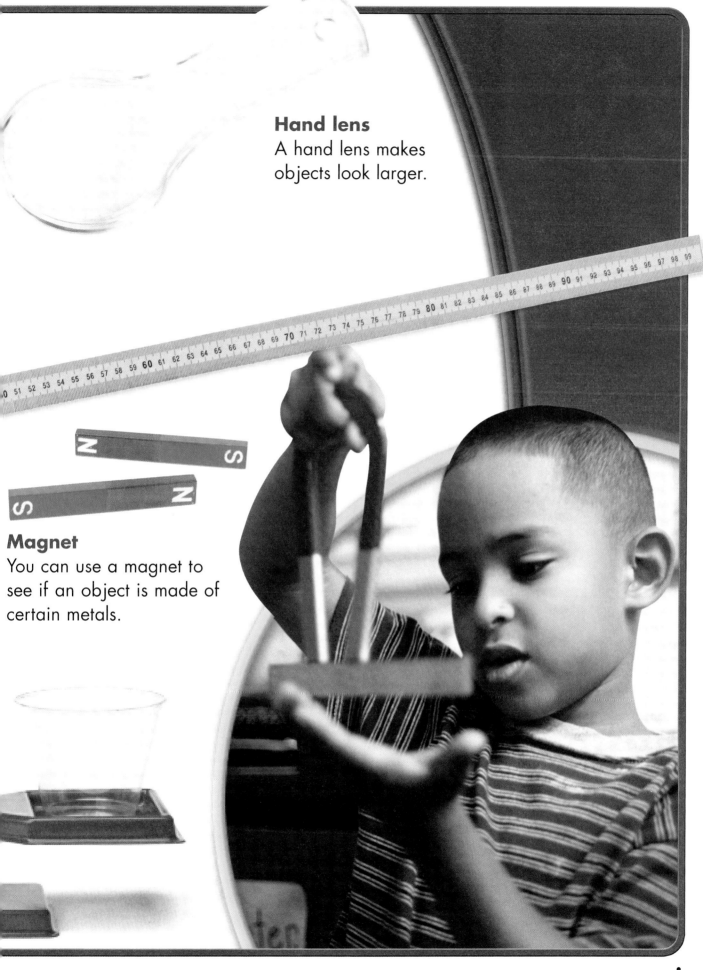

Hand lens
A hand lens makes objects look larger.

Magnet
You can use a magnet to see if an object is made of certain metals.

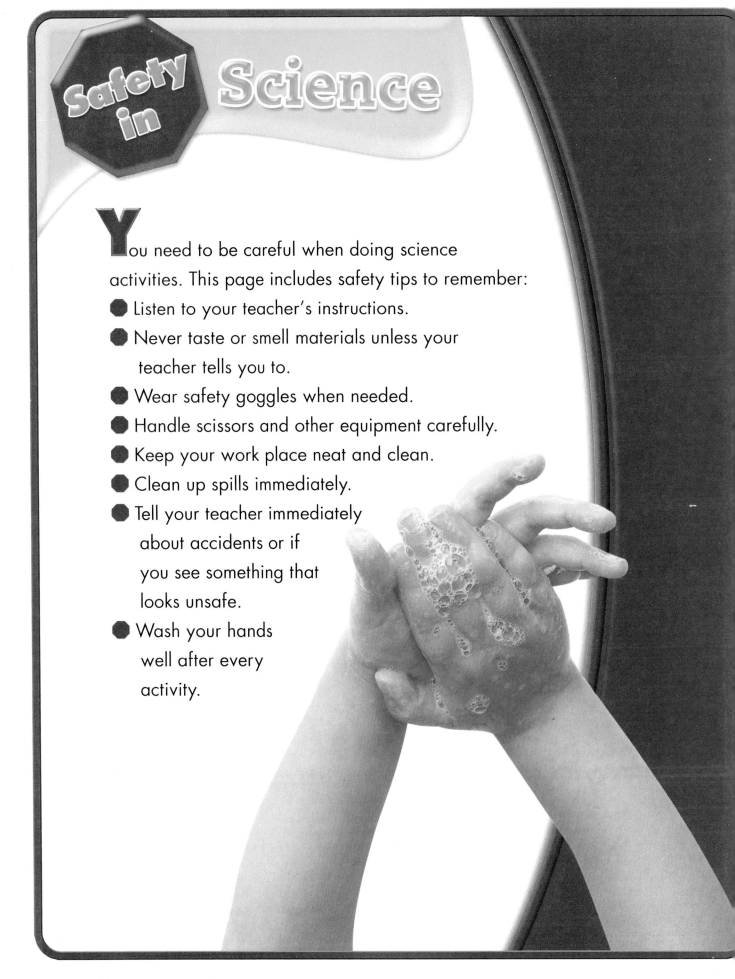

Safety in Science

You need to be careful when doing science activities. This page includes safety tips to remember:

- Listen to your teacher's instructions.
- Never taste or smell materials unless your teacher tells you to.
- Wear safety goggles when needed.
- Handle scissors and other equipment carefully.
- Keep your work place neat and clean.
- Clean up spills immediately.
- Tell your teacher immediately about accidents or if you see something that looks unsafe.
- Wash your hands well after every activity.

You Will Discover
- what makes up Earth.
- how people can help protect Earth.

Chapter 6
Land, Water, and Air

How are land, water, and air important?

sand

clay

humus

rocks

weathering

natural resource

erosion

Chapter 6
Vocabulary

minerals

Explore How can you make a model of land and water?

Materials

gloves

pan

soil

lid with water

What To Do

1 Put on your gloves.

2 Make a model. Show land and water on Earth.

What part looks like a hill?

What part looks like a lake?

Process Skills

Making a model can help you learn about Earth.

Explain Your Results
What parts of Earth do you see in your **model?**

Important Details

Important details are pictures and words that tell you about something.

Science Diagram

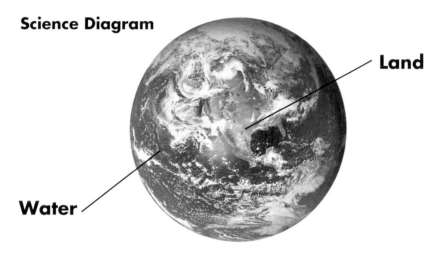

Land

Water

This is how Earth looks from space.
The blue is the water on Earth.
The brown and green are land on Earth.

Apply It!

Suppose you are going to **make a model** of Earth. What important details would you show?

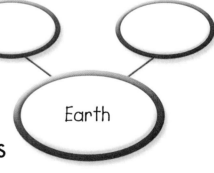

Earth

Water, Air, and Land

Sung to the tune of "I've Been Working On the Railroad"
Lyrics by Gerri Brioso & Richard Freitas/The Dovetail Group, Inc.

Earth is made of land and water.

Air is all around.

Earth is made of land and water.

And look what else I found.

Science Songs

Lesson 1

What makes up Earth?

Look at the picture.
Find the land.
Find the water.
Land and water make up the surface
of Earth.
There is more water than land on Earth.

Kinds of Land and Water

Different kinds of land and water are found on Earth.

hill

plain

A plain is flat land.
A hill is where the land gets higher.

lake

This is a lake.
A lake is water that has land all around it.

river

This is a river.
A river is water that flows through the land.

A cliff is land that is very steep.
Look at this cliff.
This cliff is next to the ocean.

✓ **Lesson Checkpoint**

1. What makes up the surface of Earth?

2. 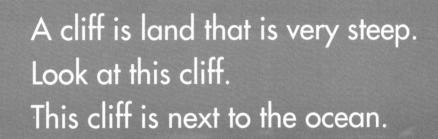 What is one **important detail** that you saw and read about a lake?

153

What are rocks and soil?

Rocks are nonliving things.
Rocks come from Earth.

Rocks can be many colors.
Some rocks feel smooth.
Some rocks feel rough.

Rocks are all different sizes and shapes.
Sand is tiny pieces of broken rock.
Big rocks are called boulders.

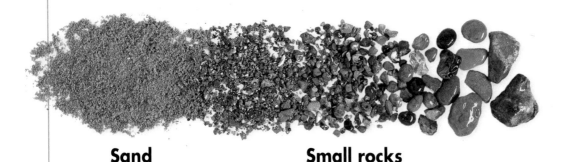

Sand   **Small rocks**

The road is made of rocks.

The fox is hiding in
the rocks.

Rocks are a natural resource.
A **natural resource** is a useful
thing that comes from nature.

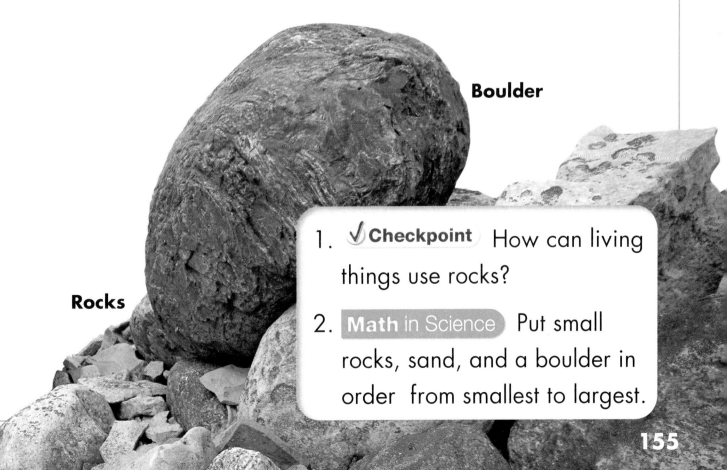

Boulder

Rocks

1. ✓Checkpoint How can living
things use rocks?

2. Math in Science Put small
rocks, sand, and a boulder in
order from smallest to largest.

155

Soil

Soil is a natural resource.
Soil may have sand, clay, and
humus in it.

Sand

Sand feels rough.
Sand is loose and easy to dig.

Clay

Clay is sticky and soft.
It is hard for plants to grow in clay.

Humus

Humus is made of parts of living
things that died.

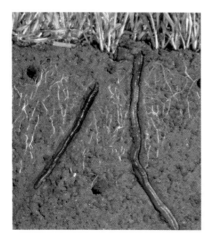

**Worms loosen the
soil. The loose soil
helps plants grow.**

**Humus in the soil
helps plants grow.**

1. What helps plants grow?

2. **Math** in Science How many rabbits are in the picture?

Look at this picture. What lives and grows in the soil?

What changes land?

Weathering can change land.
Weathering happens when rocks break apart and change. Water and ice can cause weathering. Weathering can take a long time!

Erosion can change land. **Erosion** happens when wind or water moves rocks and soil.

Roots of plants help hold the soil in place. Plants can slow down erosion.

✓ **Lesson Checkpoint**

1. What can change rocks?

2. 🎯 What is one **important detail** you saw and read about erosion?

Weathering helped change the shape, size, and color of this rock.

Crack!
Tree roots break the sidewalk as they grow. This is weathering.

Erosion is happening here. The water is washing the soil away quickly.

How can people and animals change the soil?

159

How do living things use natural resources?

Air is a natural resource.
Plants and trees need clean air to grow.
People and animals breathe air.
Some animals fly in the air.

Cars and trucks can give off harmful
materials into the air.
People can help keep the air clean.
People can walk.
People can ride bikes.

Wind is moving air. Look at how the wind blows the leaves of the trees.

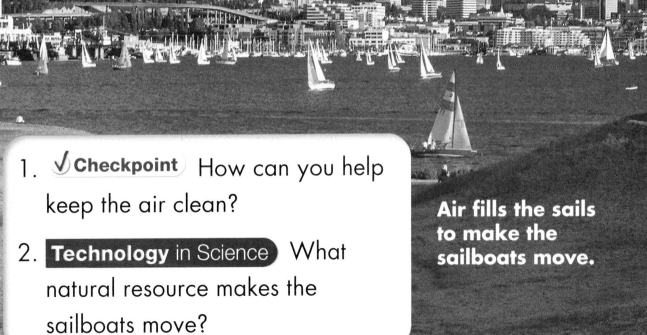

1. ✓ **Checkpoint** How can you help keep the air clean?

2. **Technology** in Science What natural resource makes the sailboats move?

Air fills the sails to make the sailboats move.

Using Water

Water is a natural resource.
Many animals live in water.
Most animals drink water.

Splish!

This crab lives in the ocean. Some people use crabs for food.

People use water for drinking. People use water for bathing and cooking food. What other ways do people use water?

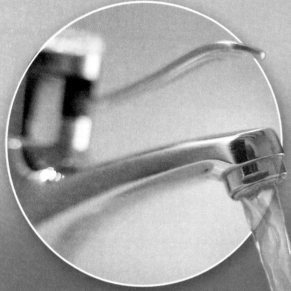

You can save water by turning the water off when brushing your teeth.

Splash! People swim and play in water.

1. ✓Checkpoint How do animals use water?

2. Writing in Science Write in your science journal. List three ways that you use water.

163

Using Land

Land is an important natural resource. The pictures show ways that people use land.

People grow food in soil. People use wood from trees to build things.

Minerals come from the land. **Minerals** are nonliving things. Minerals are found in rocks and soil. Gold, silver, and copper are minerals. People use minerals in different ways.

✓ **Lesson Checkpoint**

1. What is one way that people use land?

2. **Writing** in Science Write a sentence that describes minerals.

Carrots grow in soil. What other foods that you eat grow in soil?

Trees grow on land. Name some things made from wood.

minerals

pennies

People use copper to make pennies.

You can help keep the land clean. You can put trash in a trash can.

How can you reduce, reuse, and recycle?

You can help save Earth's land, water, and air.
You can reduce, reuse, and recycle.

Reduce means to use less.

Reuse means to use things again.

Recycle means to make old things into new things.

You can carry food in a cloth bag. This will help reduce the paper you use.

You can reuse an old jug. It can be a pot for plants.

Old papers can be recycled to make boxes.

Glass bottles can be recycled to make glass beads.

✔ Lesson Checkpoint

1. What are three ways to help save Earth's resources?

2. **Art** in Science Make a poster. Show others how to reduce, reuse, and recycle.

Investigate How are these soils different?

Materials

cups with soils

hand lens

cup with water

dropper

3 craft sticks

What to Do

① **Observe** the soils.

② **Collect Data** Draw and write about the dry soils. Use the word bank.

humus   sand   clay

③ Add water and stir.

clay

Process Skills

Recording in a chart is a way to **collect data** about soils.

4 Draw and write about the wet soils. Use the word bank.

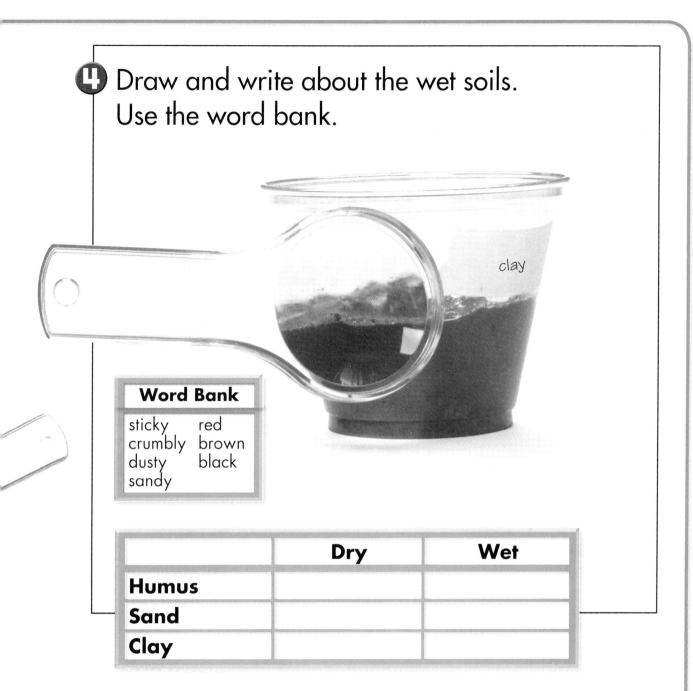

clay

Word Bank

sticky	red
crumbly	brown
dusty	black
sandy	

	Dry	Wet
Humus		
Sand		
Clay		

Explain Your Results

1. **Communicate** How did the soils change when you added water?
2. Which of the soils have you seen? Tell where.

Go Further

What is the soil like where you live? Investigate to find out.

169

Reading a Picture Graph

Look at the picture graph. It shows what the children at West School found in their school's recycling bin.

Use the picture graph to answer the questions.

What children found in their recycling bin.					
Juice Boxes	🧃	🧃	🧃		
Cans	🥫	🥫	🥫	🥫	
Paper	📄	📄			
Plastic Bottles	🍼				

1. Are there more cans or bottles in the recycling bin?
2. How many things are there to recycle in all?

Lab zone **Take-Home Activity**

Collect cans used by your family. Collect boxes used by your family. Make a picture graph. Show how many cans and boxes your family can recycle.

Vocabulary

Which picture goes with each word?

1. rocks
2. sand
3. clay
4. humus
5. erosion
6. minerals

A

B

C

D

E

F

What did you learn?

7. What is weathering?

8. Why is land an important natural resource?

9. How do you use water and air?

10. Collect Data Name things in your classroom that can be recycled or reused.

Lily's Shoebox

Lily is using a shoebox. She is using it to hold her CDs.

Shoes CDs

Important Details

11. What are two **important details** you saw and read about Lily's shoebox?

Lily's shoebox

Fill in the circle that correctly answers the question.

12. What makes up the surface of Earth?

Ⓐ sun and moon

Ⓑ water and land

Ⓒ plants and animals

Ⓓ summer and winter

13. Writing in Science Write two sentences. Tell how people can protect the land.

Satellites Help Scientists Find Fossils

NASA Landsat satellites go around Earth. Landsat satellites send information about land on Earth. This information helps some scientists find places to look for fossils.

A fossil is a part or a print of a plant or animal that lived long ago. Some fossils are found in rocks. Look at the pictures of fossils on the next page.

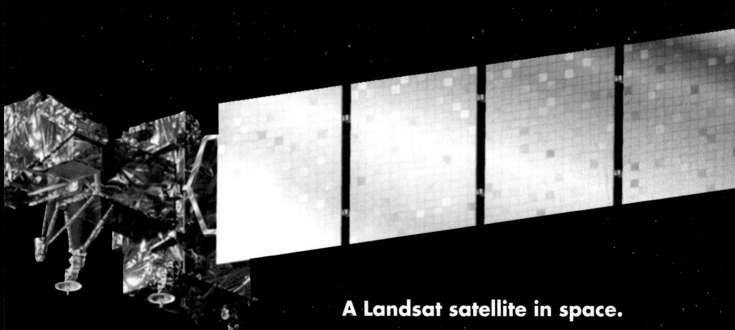

A Landsat satellite in space.

Fossils can teach us about animals that lived on Earth. Fossils can teach us about Earth's past.

This is a fossil of dinosaur eggs.

Geologist and Paleontologist
Dr. Winifred Goldring

Read Together

Winifred Goldring loved rocks and fossils when she was young. She became a geologist and a paleontologist when she grew up. A geologist studies rocks. A paleontologist studies fossils.

First, Dr. Goldring was a teacher. Then, she set up rocks and fossils for people to look at in a museum. Dr. Goldring also wrote books about rocks and fossils.

Dr. Goldring studied this National Historic Landmark called the "Grotto."

Dr. Goldring was the first female State Paleontologist of New York.

Lab zone Take-Home Activity

Collect some rocks around your neighborhood. Set up your rocks for others to see. Show your rocks to your family.

EC NTL 10 9 8 7 6 5 4

Chapter 7
Weather

You Will Discover

- what tools are used to measure weather.
- about the seasons.

Web Games
Take It to the Net
sfsuccessnet.com

Discovery Channel School
Student DVD
Discovery CHANNEL SCHOOL

online
Student Edition
sfsuccessnet.com

What are the four seasons?

season

weather

temperature

thermometer

water vapor

Water vapor is a form of water in the air.

178

Chapter 7 Vocabulary

clouds

sleet

179

Explore How can you tell when it is windy?

Materials

long and short straws

stapler

tape

plastic bag

What to Do

1 Have your teacher attach the 2 straws.

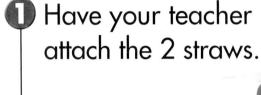

2 Tape the bag onto the straws. You made a wind sock!

3 Go outside on a windy day. **Predict** what will happen to your wind sock. Observe.

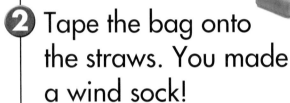

Process Skills

Predict means to tell what you think might happen.

Explain Your Results
Predict How will your wind sock act in low wind?

How to Read Science

Reading Skills

Predict

Predict means to make a guess from what you already know.

Science Story

A Windy Day

The wind is blowing. The wind helps the kites fly in the sky.

Apply It!

Predict What will happen to the kites if the wind stops blowing?

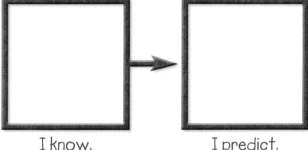

I know.   I predict.

♪ Can I Go Outside and Play?

Sung to the tune of "Oh Susannah"
Lyrics by Gerri Brioso & Richard Freitas/The Dovetail Group, Inc.

In winter it gets very cold,

And sometimes there is snow.

I need to wear a hat and gloves,

And then I'm ready to go!

Lesson 1

How can you measure weather?

Weather is what it is like outside.
Weather may change from day to day.
Weather may be windy or still.
Weather may be cloudy or sunny.
Weather may be wet or dry.

183

Weather Tools

You can use a thermometer to see what the weather is like.

A **thermometer** is a tool used to measure temperature. **Temperature** is how hot or cold something is.

All thermometers have numbers. The numbers show temperature.

Whew!
It is hot today. The temperature goes up as the air gets warmer.

Brr!
It is cold today. The temperature goes down as the air gets cooler.

Sometimes the weather is windy.
People use a tool called a wind vane.
Wind vanes tell the direction of the wind.
A wind vane points into the wind.

Sometimes the weather is rainy.
People use a rain gauge to measure
how much rain falls.

√ **Lesson Checkpoint**

1. What tool might you use to measure air temperature?

2. **Technology** in Science What tools might people use in different kinds of weather?

Whoosh!
The wind is blowing hard.

Pitter-patter
Rain is pouring down.

185

How do clouds form?

There is water in the air.
Water vapor is a form of water
in the air. You cannot see water vapor.

Clouds form when water vapor cools.
Clouds are made of tiny drops of water or
pieces of ice.

Clouds have many shapes and sizes.
Different clouds bring different kinds
of weather.

✔️**Lesson Checkpoint**

1. What makes up clouds?

2. 🎯 Observe the clouds in the sky.
   Predict the weather.

These clouds are very high in the sky. These clouds are signs of good weather.

These fluffy clouds are signs of good weather too.

These dark gray clouds are signs of storms.

Fog is made of tiny water drops. Fog is a cloud that is near the ground. It is hard to see in fog.

187

What are some kinds of wet weather?

This snake finds shelter from the rain.

Rain is one kind of wet weather. Many animals look for shelter when it rains. The animals want to stay dry. Many people look for shelter too. How can you stay dry in the rain?

These children are keeping dry in the rain.

Plants need rain.
Plants get water from rain.
Plants need water to live.

A plant needs rain to grow.

It is cold outside.
Rain may change into sleet.
Sleet is frozen rain.
Sleet is another kind of wet weather.

1. ✔ **Checkpoint** What are two kinds of wet weather?

2. **Math** in Science Make a chart. Show how many days this week had sun, clouds, or rain.

Snowy Weather

The temperature went down.
Snow began to fall.

Snow is water that freezes high in the air.
Snow falls in very cold weather.
Snow is a kind of wet weather.

These bears live where
there is a lot of snow.
These bears have thick fur.
Thick fur helps the bears
stay warm.

Look at how much snow fell during this blizzard.

A blizzard is a snowstorm.
A lot of snow falls during a blizzard.
Strong winds blow the snow.

✔ **Lesson Checkpoint**

1. What is a blizzard?

2. 🎯 **Predict** Tell what clothes you might wear if it started to snow.

Lesson 4

What are the four seasons?

A **season** is a time of year. The four seasons are spring, summer, fall, and winter. Spring comes after winter.

spring

It is warm in the spring.

summer

Summer comes after spring. Summer is warmer than spring.

The pattern of the seasons begins again.
What are the seasons like where you live?

✔ **Lesson Checkpoint**

1. Tell the four seasons in order. Begin with spring.

2. **Writing** in Science Write in your **science journal.** Tell about winter where you live.

Fall comes after summer. Fall is cooler than summer.

Winter comes after fall. Winter is the coldest season of the year.

Investigate How does the temperature change each day?

Materials

thermometer

red crayons

What to Do

1 **Measure** the temperature outside for 5 days. Measure the temperature at the same time each day.

2 **Collect Data** Show the temperature each day. Use a red crayon.

Process Skills

You can use a thermometer to **measure** temperature.

❸ Compare the temperatures.

Temperature				
Day 1	**Day 2**	**Day 3**	**Day 4**	**Day 5**

Explain Your Results

1. How can you tell which day you recorded the warmest temperatures?

2. **Interpret Data** Which day did you measure the coldest temperature?

Go Further

How does the temperature change from month to month where you live? Make a plan to find out.

Using a Bar Graph

Map Facts

Cincinnati, Ohio, usually gets about 121 cm of rain each year.

e Tools Take It to the Net
sfsuccessnet.com

Rainfall in Cincinnati, Ohio

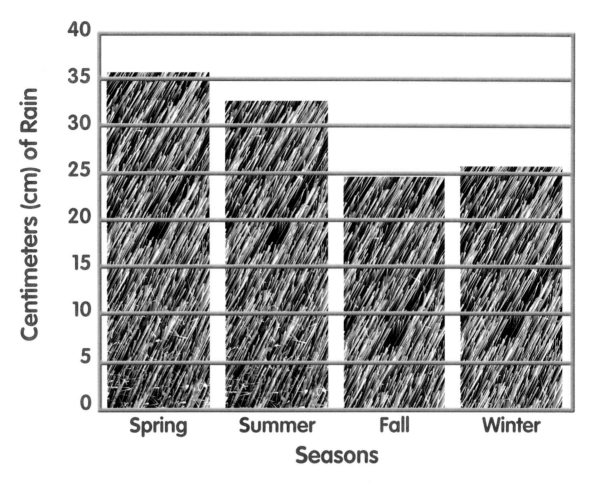

Use the bar graph to answer these questions.
1. Which season gets the most rain in Cincinnati, Ohio?
2. Which season gets the least rain in Cincinnati, Ohio?

Lab zone Take-Home Activity

Use a rain gauge to measure how much rain falls where you live each day. Make a bar graph to show how much rain falls each day in a week.

Vocabulary

Which picture goes with each word?

1. cloud

2. sleet

3. thermometer

What did you learn?

4. What is weather?

5. What tools are used to measure weather?

6. What is water vapor?

7. What is the warmest season of the year?

Process Skills

8. Predict The sky is full of dark gray clouds. Predict what the weather might be like.

Predict

9. Suppose the summer is very dry. **Predict** what might happen to this plant.

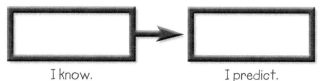

I know.   I predict.

Test Prep

Fill in the circle next to the correct answer.

10. What is used to measure temperature?
  Ⓐ rain gauge
  Ⓑ season
  Ⓒ thermometer
  Ⓓ wind vane

11. Writing in Science Write how some animals might stay warm in snowy weather.

Meteorologist

Read Together

Dr. J. Marshall Shepherd is a research meteorologist at NASA.

A meteorologist is a scientist who studies or predicts the weather. First, some meteorologists use special weather tools to collect data.

Next, some meteorologists make special maps about the weather.

Last, some meteorologists share their predictions about what the weather will be like.

Dr. Shepherd does science experiments that help us to better understand Earth and its weather.

Lab zone Take-Home Activity

Look at a weather map in a newspaper. Collect data from the map. Predict what the weather might be like tomorrow.

Unit B Test Talk

Test-Taking Strategies

Find Important Words

Choose the Right Answer

▶ Use Information from Text and Graphics

Write Your Answer

Use Information from Text and Graphics

Read the chart and text.

Temperature

Day	Temperature
Monday	10 degrees Celsius
Tuesday	20 degrees Celsius
Wednesday	25 degrees Celsius
Thursday	15 degrees Celsius
Friday	10 degrees Celsius

Juan made a chart of the temperature for five days. Wednesday was the warmest day.

Use the information in the chart and in the text to answer the question.

What was the temperature on the warmest day of the week?

(A) 10 degrees Celsius

(B) 15 degrees Celsius

(C) 25 degrees Celsius

(D) 20 degrees Celsius

The text tells what day was the warmest. Look at the chart to see what the temperature was on that day.

Unit B Wrap-Up

Chapter 6

How are land, water, and air important?

- Land and water make up the surface of Earth.
- Land, water, and air are important natural resources.

Chapter 7

What are the four seasons?

- The four seasons are spring, summer, fall, and winter.

Performance Assessment

Make a Poster

- Find pictures in a magazine of people using water.

- Cut the pictures out.

- Make a poster using your pictures. Tell about all the ways that you can use water.

Read More About Earth Science!

Look for books like these in your library.

Full Inquiry

Experiment Does the Sun warm land or water faster?

The sunlight warms Earth's land and water during the day. Does the sunlight warm land and water in the same way?

Materials

cup with water and cup with soil

2 thermometers

lamp

Ask a question.

Does sunlight warm the land or water faster?

Make a hypothesis.

Will a cup of soil warm faster than a cup of water? Tell what you think.

Plan a fair test.

Make sure the lamp is placed evenly above both cups.

Do your test.

Process Skills

You **plan a fair test** in an experiment when you choose the one thing that you will change.

1 Put one thermometer in the soil. Put the other thermometer in the water.

The soil is like land.

2 Wait for 30 minutes.
Record the temperatures.

3 Place the lamp so the light shines on both cups.

4 Wait 1 hour.
Record the temperatures.

5 Turn the light off.

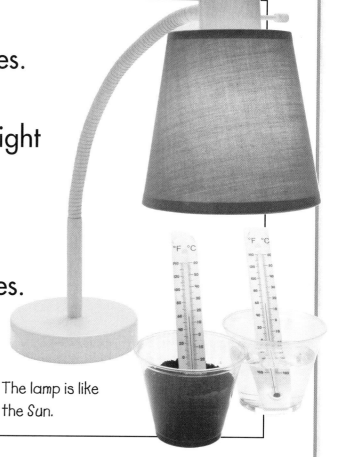

The lamp is like the *Sun*.

Collect and record data.

	Temperature at start	Temperature after 1 hour
Soil		
Water		

Tell your conclusion.

Did soil or water warm faster? Do you think the Sun warms land or water faster? Why do you think so?

Go Further

What if the cups were under the lamp for 2 hours? Try it and find out.

Wind

by Ivy O. Eastwick

Nobody knows
where the Wind goes—
it comes with a flutter
it goes with a gust,
it comes when it will
and it goes where it must
but—
where it goes,
nobody knows.

Full Inquiry

Using Scientific Methods
1. Ask a question.
2. Make a hypothesis.
3. Plan a fair test.
4. Do your test.
5. Collect and record data.
6. Tell your conclusion.
7. Go further.

Idea 1
Comparing Temperature

Plan a project. Find out how close predicted temperatures are to actual temperatures.

Idea 2
Erosion

Plan a project. Find out how long it takes erosion to happen in sand, soil, and clay.

Sand   **Clay**   **Soil**

EC NTL 1098765 4

Metric and Customary Measurement

Science uses the metric system to measure things. Metric measurement is used around the world. Here is how different metric measurements compare to customary measurement.

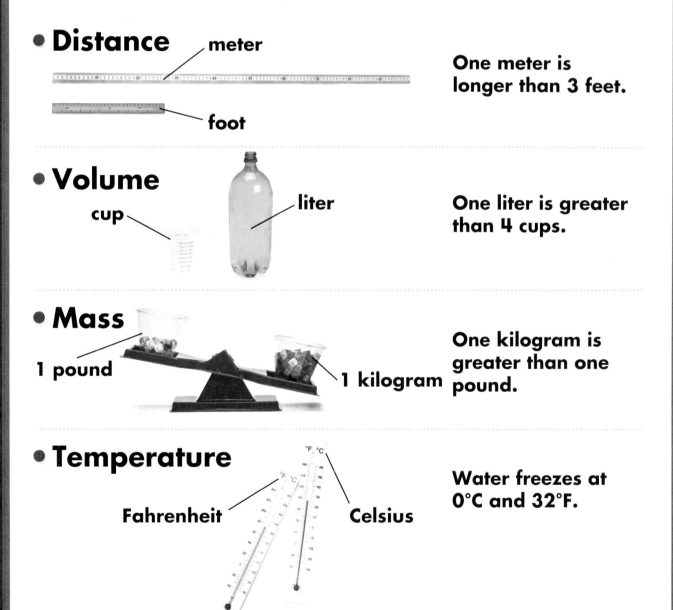

- **Distance**

  meter

  foot

  One meter is longer than 3 feet.

- **Volume**

  cup

  liter

  One liter is greater than 4 cups.

- **Mass**

  1 pound

  1 kilogram

  One kilogram is greater than one pound.

- **Temperature**

  Fahrenheit

  Celsius

  Water freezes at 0°C and 32°F.

Glossary

The glossary uses letters and signs to show how words are pronounced. The mark ′ is placed after a syllable with a primary or heavy accent. The mark ′ is placed after a syllable with a secondary or lighter accent.

To hear these words pronounced, listen to the AudioText CD.

alike (ə līk′) How things are the same. The two foxes look **alike**. (pages 5, 53, 213)

antennae (an ten′ē) Feelers that help some animals know what is around them. **Antennae** help the crab feel, smell, and taste. (page 56)

Antennae

attract (ə trakt′) Attract means to pull toward. Magnets **attract** some objects. (page 256)

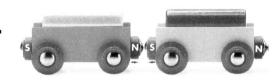

battery (bat′ər ē) Something that stores energy. The toy robot uses a **battery** to move. (page 293)

camouflage (kam′ə fläzh) A color or shape that makes an animal or plant hard to see. **Camouflage** helps the rabbit stay safe in its environment. (page 62)

cause (kȯz) Why something happens. Taking out the bottom block can cause the tower to fall. (pages 245, 254)

clay (klā) A soft part of soil that looks like mud, is sticky when wet, and is hard when dry. The **clay** felt sticky when Tanya touched it. (page 156)

cloud (kloud) A form in the air made of many tiny drops of water or pieces of ice when water vapor cools. We watched the fluffy, white **clouds** float overhead. (page 186)

desert (dez´ərt) A desert is a very dry habitat that gets little rain. Many **deserts** are hot during the day. (page 38)

different (dif´ər ənt) How things are not the same. The dogs are different colors. (pages 5, 53, 96, 213)

dissolve (di zolv´) To spread throughout a liquid. Salt will **dissolve** in water. (page 225)

draw conclusions

(dró kən klü′zhənz) When you decide something about what you see or read. You can **draw** a **conclusion** about what the shark will eat. (pages 117, 277)

effect

effect (ə fekt′) What happens. The **effect** of pulling out the bottom block was that the blocks fell down. (pages 245, 254)

electricity

electricity (i lek′tris′ə tē) Makes things work. The streetlight uses **electricity** to shine. (page 290)

energy

energy (en′ər jē) Something that can change things. Sunlight is a form of **energy** from the Sun. (page 282)

erosion (i rō′zhən) Happens when wind or water moves rocks and soil from one place to another. **Erosion** washed away the soil near the stream. (page 158)

evaporate (i vap′ə rāt′) To change from a liquid to a gas. The water on the ground quickly **evaporated** when the Sun came out. (page 228)

flower (flou′ər) The part of a plant that makes seeds. Our garden has many colorful **flowers**. (page 69)

food chain (füd chān) The way food passes from one living thing to another. All living things are connected through **food chains.** (page 125)

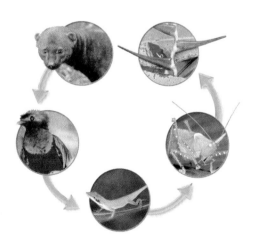

force (fôrs) A push or pull that makes objects move. The children used **force** to move the sled. (page 247)

forest (fôr′ist) A habitat with many trees and other types of plants. Many animals live in the **forest**. (page 31)

fuel (fyü′əl) Anything that is burned to make heat or power. People use gasoline as a **fuel** for cars. (page 290)

G

gas (gas) A kind of matter that can change size and shape. The bubbles are full of **gas**. (page 221)

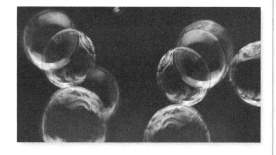

gravity (grav′ə tē) A force that pulls things toward the ground. **Gravity** pulls falling leaves toward the ground. (page 247)

H

habitat (hab′ə tat) A place where plants and animals live. A deer lives in a forest **habitat**. (page 31)

heat (hēt) Moves from warmer places and objects to cooler places and objects. The **heat** from the campfire kept us warm. (page 279)

humus (hyü′ məs) A nonliving material made up of parts of living things that have died. Grandmother adds **humus** to the soil to help her plants grow. (page 156)

important details (im pôrt′nt di tālz′) Pictures and words that tell you about something. We looked for **important details** in the book we were reading. (pages 149, 317)

inclined plane (in klīnd′ plān) A simple machine that is high at one end and low at the other. It helps move things up and down. The builders used an **inclined plane** to help move the wood. (page 359)

larva (lär′və) A young insect that has a different shape from the adult. A butterfly **larva** is called a caterpillar. (page 92)

leaf (lēf) A part of a plant that makes food for the plant. A **leaf** fell from the rose bush. (page 69)

lever (lev′ər) A simple machine that can be used to lift something. Denny used a **lever** to lift the nail out. (page 358)

life cycle (līf sī′kəl) The changes that take place as a plant or an animal grows and changes. The **life cycle** of a frog includes an egg, a tadpole, and a grown frog. (page 90)

liquid (lik′wid) Matter that takes the shape of its container. Water is a **liquid**. (page 220)

living (liv′ing) Things that are alive and can grow and change. The butterfly is a **living** thing. (page 7)

M

magnet (mag′nit) An object that attracts some kinds of metal. A **magnet** can pull an object made of iron without touching it. (pages 256, 258)

marsh (märsh) A wetland habitat. Many different plants and animals live in a **marsh**. (page 126)

mass (mas) Amount of matter in an object. Everything made of matter has **mass**. (page 215)

matter (mat′er) Anything that takes up space. Everything around you is made of **matter**. (page 215)

mineral (min′ər əl) A nonliving material that can be found in rocks and soil. Copper is a **mineral**. (page 164)

Moon (mün) An object in the sky that moves around Earth. The **Moon** was shining brightly in the night sky. (page 326)

natural resource

(nach′ər əl ri sôrs′) A useful thing that comes from nature. Rocks are a **natural resource**. (page 155)

nonliving (non liv′ing) Things that are not alive, don't grow, and don't change on their own. Tables and chairs are **nonliving** things. (page 14)

ocean (ō′shən) A large, deep habitat that has salt water. Some fish live in an **ocean** habitat. (page 36)

oxygen (ok′sə jən) A gas in the air that plants and animals need to live. Most living things need **oxygen** to live. (page 121)

planet (plan′it) A large body of matter that moves around the Sun. Earth is one of the nine **planets**. (page 324)

pole (pōl) At the end of some magnets. The north **pole** of one magnet will attract the south **pole** of another magnet. (page 256)

predict (pri dikt′) To make a guess from what you already know. See the clouds high in the sky. What do you **predict** the weather will be like? (page 181)

pulley (púl′ē) A simple machine that uses a wheel and rope to move things up and down. The workers used a **pulley** to move the wood. (page 358)

pupa (pyü′pə) The step after larva in some insects' life cycle. The hard covering of the **pupa** protects the caterpillar while it changes into a butterfly. (page 92)

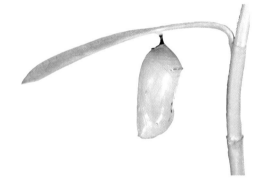

R

rain forest (rān fôr′ist) A habitat that gets a lot of rain. Plants with large green leaves grow in the **rain forest**. (page 122)

repel (ri pel′) To push away. The north poles of two magnets placed together will **repel** each other. (page 257)

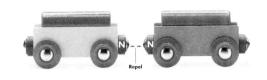

rocks (roks) Nonliving things that come from Earth. José collects **rocks**. (page 154)

root (rüt) Part of a plant that holds the plant in place and takes in water for the plant. We covered the **roots** of the rose plant with soil. (page 68)

rotation (rō tā′shən) The act of turning around and around. Earth's **rotation** causes day and night. (page 322)

sand (sand) Tiny pieces of broken rock. We made castles of **sand** at the beach. (page 154)

screw (skrü) A simple machine used to hold things together. A **screw** was used to keep the two wooden boards together. (page 358)

season (sē′zn) One of the four parts of the year. Winter is my favorite **season**. (page 192)

seed coat (sēd kōt) The protective shell that covers and protects a seed. The **seed coat** breaks open as the plant begins to grow. (page 98)

seedling (sēd′ling) A very young plant. Rafiq planted the **seedling** in his yard. (page 98)

shadow (shad′ō) A dark shape made when something blocks light. The doll made a **shadow** on the floor. (page 286)

shelter (shel′tər) A safe place for animals and people. This wolf pup uses an old log for **shelter**. (page 12)

simple machine (sim′pəl mə shēn′) A tool with few or no moving parts that does work. The wheel and axle of this wheelbarrow is a **simple machine**. (page 356)

sleet (slēt) Sleet is frozen rain. **Sleet** made the roads very slippery. (page 189)

solid (sol′id) A kind of matter that takes up space and has its own shape. A wooden block is a **solid**. (page 218)

speed (spēd) How quickly or slowly something moves. The car moved at a very fast **speed**. (page 250)

star (stär) A big ball of hot gas. **Stars** shine brightly in the night sky. (pages 319, 324)

stem (stem) The part of a plant that carries water to the leaves. The rose's **stem** has sharp thorns. (page 68)

Sun (sun) A big ball of hot gas that makes the day sky bright. The light from the **Sun** warms the Earth. (page 319)

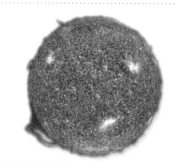

tadpole (tad′pōl′) A very young frog. Rosie caught **tadpoles** in the pond. (page 87)

technology (tek nol′ə jē) The use of scientific knowledge to solve problems. A computer is a machine that uses **technology**. (page 343)

telescope (tel′ə skōp) Makes things that are far away look closer and brighter. We use a **telescope** to look at the stars in the sky. (page 324)

temperature (tem′per ə chər) How hot or cold something is. The **temperature** can be very hot in the desert. (page 184)

thermometer (thər mom′ə tər) A tool that measures temperature. We looked at the **thermometer** to see how cold it was outside. (page 184)

vibrate (vī′brāt) To move back and forth very fast. The banjo strings **vibrate** to make sounds. (page 260)

water vapor (wȯ′tər vā′pər) A form of water in the air. You cannot see **water vapor**. (page 186)

weather (weᴛʜ′ ər) What it is like outside. I like to make snowmen when the **weather** outside is cold and snowy. (page 183)

weathering (weᴛʜ′ər ing) The breaking apart and changing of rocks. **Weathering** can change the shape, size, and color of rocks. (page 158)

wedge (wej) A simple machine used to push things apart. The farmer used a shovel as a **wedge** to break up the soil. (page 356)

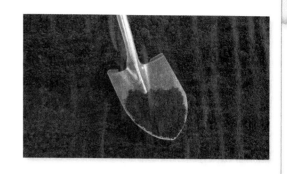

wetland (wet′land′) A habitat that is covered with water. Tanya saw a bullfrog when she visited the **wetland** near her home. (page 34)

wheel and axle (hwēl and ak′səl) A simple machine used to move things. A wheelbarrow has a **wheel and axle**. (page 356)

Index

This index lists the pages on which topics appear in this book.
Page number after a *p* refer to a photograph or drawing.

Credits

Text

"The Frog on the Log" by Ilo Orleans from *Read-Aloud Rhymes for the Very Young* selected by Jack Prelutsky. Copyright ©1986 by Alfred A. Knopf.

"Wind" from *Some Folks Like Cats and Other Poems* by Ivy O. Eastwick. Reprinted by permission of Boyds Mills Press.

"Merry-Go-Round" from *I Like Machinery* by Dorothy Baruch.

"Taking Off" from *Very Young Verses*, edited by Barbara Peck Geismer and Antoinette Brown Suter. Copyright ©1945 by Houghton Mifflin company; Copyright ©Renewed 1972 by Barbara P. Geismer and Antoinette Brown Suter. Reprinted by permission of Houghton Mifflin Company. All Rights Reserved.

Illustrations

31-32, 34, 36, 38 Robert Hynes; 108-109 Cheryl Mendenhall; 322 Henk Dawson.

Photographs

Every effort has been made to secure permission and provide appropriate credit for photographic material. The publisher deeply regrets any omission and pledges to correct errors called to its attention in subsequent editions.

Unless otherwise acknowledged, all photographs are the property of Scott Foresman, a division of Pearson Education.

Photo locators denoted as follows: Top (T), Center (C), Bottom (B), Left (L), Right (R), Background (Bkgd).

Cover: (C) ©Tui De Roy/Minden Pictures, (Bkgd) ©Tim Davis/Corbis, (BL) Getty Images.

Front Matter: ii ©DK Images; iii (TR, B) ©DK Images; v ©DK Images; vi (B) ©DK Images, (CL) Corbis; vii Getty Images; viii (CL) Digital Vision, (BC) ©DK Images; ix (CR) ©Michael and Patricia Fogden/Corbis, (B) ©DK Images; x (TL, CL, B) ©Michael & Patricia Fogden/Corbis, (BR) ©Rick and Nora Bowers/Visuals Unlimited; xii (CL) ©Richard Price/Getty Images, (CL) ©Thomas Kitchin/Tom Stack & Associates, Inc.; xiii (CR) Stephen Oliver/©DK Images, (CR) Getty Images; xiv (CL) Getty Images, (B) ©DK Images; xv ©Frank Siteman/PhotoEdit; xvi ©Stone/Getty Images; xvii Courtesy of the London Toy and Model Museum/Paddington, London/©DK Images; xviii (CL) NASA Image Exchange, (CL) ©Roger Ressmeyer/Corbis; xix ©Lowell Georgia/Corbis; xx ©DK Images; xxii ©Douglas Faulkner/Photo Researchers, Inc.; xxiii ©William Harrigan/Lonely Planet Images; xxiv ©William Harrigan/Lonely Planet Images; xxv (BC) ©John Pontier/Animals Animals/Earth Scenes, (TR) ©Ames/NASA; xxix ©Ed Bock/Corbis; xxxi ©Little Blue Wolf Productions/Corbis; xxxii ©Andy Crawford/DK Images.

Unit A: Divider: ©Wayne R. Bilenduke/Getty Images; 1 (C) ©Sumio Harada/Minden Pictures, (TR) ©Royalty-Free/Corbis; 2 (B) Corbis, (T) ©Pat O'Hara/Corbis; 3 ©Mary Kate Denny/PhotoEdit; 5 (Bkgd) ©Pat O'Hara/Corbis, (C) ©Royalty-Free/Corbis, (TR) ©DK Images; 6 ©Pat O'Hara/Corbis; 7 (BR) ©Darrell Gulin/Corbis, (TR) ©DK Images; 8 (TR) ©Photowood, Inc./Corbis, (TL) Getty Images; 9 (TL) ©Manoj Shah/Animals Animals/Earth Scenes, (BR) ©J. & B. Photographers/Animals Animals/Earth Scenes; 10 (BL) ©Roy Morsch/Corbis, (TL) Digital Vision; 11 ©Guy Edwardes/Getty Images; 12 (BL) ©Darrell Gulin/Corbis, (C) Corbis, (TL) ©DK Images; 13 ©Dan Guravich/Corbis; 14 ©Mary Kate Denny/PhotoEdit; 16 (TL, C) ©DK Images; 17 Brand X Pictures; 22 (TC) ©Manoj Shah/Animals Animals/Earth Scenes, (B) ©J. & B. Photographers/Animals Animals/Earth Scenes; 23 (TR) ©Darrell Gulin/Corbis, (CL, C) ©DK Images; 24 (TL) Alan Schroeder/Courtesy of Sonia Ortega, (B) ©John Bova/Photo Researchers, Inc.; **Chapter 2:** 25 (C) Getty Images, (TR) ©Stephen Dalton/Photo Researchers, Inc.; 26 (C) ©W. Perry Conway/Corbis, (BL) ©Daniel J. Cox/Natural Exposures, (BR) ©David Samuel Robbins/Corbis; 27 (BR) ©Yva Momatiuk/John Eastcott/Minden Pictures, (BL) Digital Vision; 29 (Bkgd) ©W. Perry Conway/Corbis, (TR, C) ©DK Images; 30 ©W. Perry Conway/Corbis; 31 (BR) ©Taxi/Getty Images, (TR) ©Jeremy Thomas/Natural Visions; 32 (TL) ©Jeremy Thomas/Natural Visions, (BL) ©Jeffrey Lepore/Photo Researchers, Inc., (CR) ©Daniel J. Cox/Natural Exposures; 33 ©Daniel J. Cox/Natural Exposures; 34 (BC) ©Steve Maslowski/Photo Researchers, Inc., (TL) Brand X Pictures; 35 (C) ©David Samuel Robbins/Corbis, (BR) ©Joe McDonald/Corbis, (TR) ©Stone/Getty Images, (CR) Getty Images; 36 (CR) Digital Vision, (TL) ©Stone/Getty Images; 37 (CR) ©Flip Nicklin/Minden Pictures, (TR) Getty Images, (BR) ©Photographer's Choice/Getty Images; 38 (TL) ©Photographer's Choice/Getty Images, (BL) ©DK Images; 39 (BC) ©Yva Momatiuk/John Eastcott/Minden Pictures, (TC) ©Jose Fuste Raga/Corbis; 40 ©Yva Momatiuk/John Eastcott/Minden Pictures, (TR) ©Gerry Ellis/Minden Pictures; 42 (BC) ©Nigel J. Dennis/NHPA Limited, (T) ©Art Wolfe/Stone/Getty Images; 44 (TR, BR) ©Daniel J. Cox/Natural Exposures, (CL) ©David Samuel Robbins/Corbis, (CR) ©Yva Momatiuk/John Eastcott/Minden Pictures, (TR) Digital Vision; 45 (C) ©Robert Lubeck/Animals Animals/Earth Scenes, (TR) Brand X Pictures; 46 NASA; 47 (TR) Getty Images, (CL) ©Porterfield/Chickering/Photo Researchers, Inc., (BR) ©Doug Perrine/DRK Photo; 48 (BC) ©Operation Migration, Inc.; **Chapter 3:** 49 (TL) ©DK Images, (C) ©Michael Patrick O'Neill/NHPA Limited; 50 (BL) ©Richard K. LaVal/Animals Animals/Earth Scenes, (BR) ©T. Kitchin and V. Hurst/NHPA Limited, (C) Digital Vision; 51 (BR) ©Jeff Lepore/Photo Researchers, Inc., (BL) ©J.P. Ferrero/Jacana/Photo Researchers, Inc.; 53 (Bkgd) Digital Vision, (CL) Corel, (CR) ©Lynn Stone/Index Stock Imagery, (TR) ©Helen Williams/Photo Researchers, Inc.; ©54 David Fritts/Stone/Getty Images; 55 (BR) ©Steve Coombs/Photo Researchers, Inc., (TR) Getty Images; 56 (B) ©DK Images, (TL, C) ©B. Jones and M. Shimlock/NHPA Limited; 58 (TL, BL) ©Helen Williams/Photo Researchers, Inc., (BR) ©DK Images; 59 ©Noboru Komine/Photo Researchers, Inc.; 60 (CR) ©Mitsuaki Iwago/Minden Pictures, (TR) Digital Vision, (B) ©S. Purdy Matthews/Stone/Getty Images, (TL) ©Ana Laura Gonzalez/Animals

Animals/Earth Scenes; 61 ©Art Wolfe/Getty Images; 62 (BL) ©Stephen Krasemann/Stone, (CR) ©T. Kitchin and V. Hurst/NHPA Limited, (TL) ©Richard K. LaVal/Animals Animals/Earth Scenes; 63 (T) ©Richard K. LaVal/Animals Animals/Earth Scenes, (B) ©J.P. Ferrero/Jacana/Photo Researchers, Inc.; 64 (BC) ©Dante Fenolio/Photo Researchers, Inc., (TL, BC) ©DK Images; 65 (C) ©John Warden/Stone/Getty Images, (CR) ©Tom and Pat Leeson/Photo Researchers, Inc.; 66 (CR) ©DK Images, (TL) ©Jerry Young/©DK Images, (CL) ©Virginia Neefus/Animals Animals/Earth Scenes; 67 ©Chase Swift/Corbis; 70 (BR) ©Tom & Pat Leeson/Photo Researchers, Inc., (CL) Getty Images, (TL, CR) ©DK Images, (BL) ©Alan and Sandy Carey/Getty Images; 71 (CL) ©John Eastcott and Yva Momatiuk/NGS Image Collection, (BL) ©Ed Reschke/Peter Arnold, Inc., (CR, BR) ©DK Images; 72 (TL, C) ©DK Images; 73 (C, CR) ©DK Images; 74 (TR) ©H. H./Getty Images, (TC) Getty Images; 76 (Bkgd) ©Arctic National Wildlife Refuge/Getty Images, (CR) ©Art Wolfe/Getty Images, (B) ©S. Purdy Matthews/Stone/Getty Images; 77 (CR) ©Virginia Neefus/Animals Animals/Earth Scenes, (TR, BR) ©DK Images, (CR) ©Stephen Krasemann/Stone, (CC) ©Helen Williams/Photo Researchers, Inc.; 78 (CR) ©J.P. Ferrero/Jacana/Photo Researchers, Inc., (BR) ©Darrell Gulin/Corbis, (C) ©DK Images; 79 (C) Photo 24/Brand X Pictures, (CR) ©Ralph A. Clevenger/Corbis, (TR) ©DK Images; 80 (BL) ©JSC/NASA, (BR, Bkgd) NASA; **Chapter 4:** 81 ©Allen Russell/Index Stock Imagery; 82 (TL, C, BL) ©DK Images, (BR) ©Michael and Patricia Fogden/Corbis; 83 (BR) ©David Young-Wolff/PhotoEdit, (CR, BC) ©DK Images, (BL) ©George D. Lepp/Corbis; 85 (TR, C, CL) ©DK Images, (CR) Odds Farm Park/©DK Images, (Bkgd) ©Stephen Dalton/NHPA Limited; 86 ©Stephen Dalton/NHPA Limited; 87 (TR, CR, BR) ©DK Images; 88 (TL, C, B) ©DK Images; 89 ©DK Images; 90 (TR, B) ©DK Images, (TL) ©Geoff Brightling/©DK Images; 91 ©DK Images; 92 (T) ©George D. Lepp/Corbis, (B) ©Michael and Patricia Fogden/Corbis, (TL) ©DK Images; 93 (BL) George D. Lepp/Corbis, (T) ©DK Images; 94 (CR) ©T. Wiewandt/DRK Photo, (B) ©Joseph T. Collins/Photo Researchers, Inc., (TL) ©DK Images; 95 (TL) ©Jane Burton/Bruce Coleman, Inc., (C) ©Norbert Wu/Minden Pictures; 96 (BL) ©Pam Francis/Getty Images, (CR) ©Pat Doyle/Corbis; 97 (TR) ©George D. Lepp/Corbis, (B) ©Bruce Ando/Index Stock Imagery; 98 Derek Hall/©DK Images; 99 ©DK Images; 100 (TL) Matthew Ward/©DK Images, (BL) ©David Young-Wolff/PhotoEdit; 101 (BR) ©Bill Ross/Corbis, (TC) ©DK Images; 102 (B) ©DK Images, (CL) ©A. Riedmiller/Peter Arnold, Inc.; 103 ©DK Images; 104 (CL, CC, CR) Brand X Pictures, (BL, BR) ©DK Images; 105 (TR) ©Stephen Dalton/Photo Researchers, Inc., (B) ©Royalty-Free/Corbis; 106 ©Steve Terrill/Corbis; 110 (TR) ©David Young-Wolff/PhotoEdit, (TC) ©George D. Lepp/Corbis, (CL) ©Michael and Patricia Fogden/Corbis, (TL, CR) ©DK Images, (BR) ©Nicolas Granier/Peter Arnold, Inc.; 111 (TR) ©DK Images, (CL, CR) ©Jeff Foott/Bruce Coleman Collection, (C) ©Daniel W. Gotshall/Seapics; 112 ©Ed Bock/Corbis; **Chapter 5:** 113 (C) ©Jonathan Blair/Corbis, (TR) ©David Aubrey/Corbis, (BC) ©Clive Druett/Papilio/Corbis; 114 (BR) ©Gary Braasch/Corbis, (C) ©Michael & Patricia Fogden/Corbis, (T) ©Ken Lucas/Visuals Unlimited; 115 ©Hal Horwitz/Corbis; 117 (C) Getty Images, (TR, Bkgd) ©Michael & Patricia

Fogden/Corbis; 118 ©Michael & Patricia Fogden/Corbis; 119 ©Michael & Patricia Fogden/Minden Pictures; 122 (B, BL) ©Michael & Patricia Fogden/Corbis, (TL) ©Michael Fogden/Animals Animals/Earth Scenes, (BR) ©Rick and Nora Bowers/Visuals Unlimited; 123 ©Kevin Schafer/NHPA Limited; 124 (TL) ©Michael & Patricia Fogden/Corbis, (BL) ©Kevin Schafer/NHPA Limited, (B) ©Steve Kaufman/Corbis; 125 (C) ©Rick and Nora Bowers/Visuals Unlimited, (CR) ©Kevin Schafer/NHPA Limited, (BR) ©Michael & Patricia Fogden/Corbis, (TR) ©Steve Kaufman/Corbis; 126 (B) ©Sue A. Thompson/Visuals Unlimited, (TL) ©Royalty-Free/Corbis; 127 ©David A. Northcott/Corbis; 128 (C) ©David A. Northcott/Corbis, (TC) ©Rick Poley/Visuals Unlimited, (TL) ©David A. Ponton/Mira, (TR) ©William J. Weber/Visuals Unlimited, (B) ©Sue A. Thompson/Visuals Unlimited; 129 (TC) ©Ted Levin/Animals Animals/Earth Scenes, (TL) ©Royalty-Free/Corbis, (CR) ©James Allen/Bruce Coleman, Inc.; 132 (TC) ©Michael & Patricia Fogden/Corbis, (C) ©John Shaw/Tom Stack & Associates, Inc.; 133 (TL) ©Michael & Patricia Fogden/Corbis, (CL) ©John Gerlach/Visuals Unlimited, (C) ©Tim Wright/Corbis, (C) ©William J. Weber/Visuals Unlimited, (CR) Getty Images, (CR) ©Michael Sewell/Peter Arnold, Inc., (CL) ©DK Images; 134 (TR, CL, C) ©Michael & Patricia Fogden/Corbis, (CR) ©Rick and Nora Bowers/Visuals Unlimited, (CR) ©Kevin Schafer/NHPA Limited, (TC) ©Hal Horwitz/Corbis, (BR) ©Jonathan Blair/Corbis; 135 (TR) ©David Aubrey/Corbis, (CR) Getty Images; 136 (BL) ©Kate Bennett Mendz/Animals Animals/Earth Scenes, (T, TC, C, R) Jerry Young/©DK Images, (TL, CR, CL, BR) ©DK Images; 138 (TL) ©Pat O'Hara/Corbis, (CL) ©W. Perry Conway/Corbis, (CL) ©David Fritts/Stone/Getty Images, (CL) ©Stephen Dalton/NHPA Limited, (BL) ©Michael & Patricia Fogden/Corbis; 140 ©Ian Beames/Ecoscene/Corbis; 142 ©John Watkins/Frank Lane Picture Agency/Corbis; 144 (Bkgd) ©Gerry Ellis/Minden Pictures, (TC) ©Breck P. Kent/Animals Animals/Earth Scenes, (BC) Corbis.

Unit B: Divider: ©Hiroyuki Matsumoto/Getty Images; **Chapter 6:** 145 (C) ©Steve Raymer/NGS Image Collection, (BR) ©Paul Chesley/NGS Image Collection; 146 (TL, BL) ©Barry L. Runk/Grant Heilman Photography, (BR) ©Garry D. McMichael/Photo Researchers, Inc., (CR) ©Richard Price/Getty Images, (CL) ©DK Images; 147 ©DK Images; 149 (Bkgd) ©Richard Price/Getty Images, (C) NASA; 150 ©Richard Price/Getty Images; 151 ©Thomas Kitchin/Tom Stack & Associates, Inc.; 152 (TR) Silver Burdett Ginn, (BR) ©J. Jangoux/Photo Researchers, Inc., (TL) ©Calvin Larsen/Photo Researchers, Inc., (C) ©Craig Aurness/Corbis; 153 ©Steve Dunwell/Getty Images; 154 (TL, B) ©DK Images; 155 (TL) ©Galen Rowell/Corbis, (TR) ©W. Perry Conway/Corbis, (B) ©J. Eastcott Film/NGS Image Collection; 156 (BL) ©J. P. Ferrero/Jacana/Photo Researchers, Inc., (BR) Getty Images, (C, CR) ©Barry L. Runk/Grant Heilman Photography, (TL, TC) ©DK Images; 157 ©Steve Shott/DK Images; 158 ©DK Images; 159 (TR) ©Barry L. Runk/Grant Heilman Photography, (TL) ©Michael Marten/Photo Researchers, Inc., (BL) ©Garry D. McMichael/Photo Researchers, Inc., (BR) ©Jeffrey Greenberg/Photo Researchers, Inc.; 160 (TL) Brand X Pictures, (BC) ©Jim Erickson/Corbis; 161 (B) ©Philip James Corwin/Corbis, (T)